The COMMON GROUND

Bible Study:

BECOMING A PEACEMAKER IN A POLARIZED WORLD

THE COMMON GROUND BIBLE STUDY SERIES

BY DR. MING WANG & DR. RICE BROOCKS

Cover Design: Eduardo Rodriguez
Interior Design: BookBaby
Interior Editing: Chartwell Literary Group
Book Development: Addison Tweedy

ISBN: 978-1-09839-306-9

CONTENTS

WHY THIS BIBLE STUDY SERIES?

Finding common ground with others has always been a priority for me since becoming a follower of Christ in my third year of university studies. Building relational bridges to others, especially with those from other cultures, has taken me to more than forty countries with the gospel of Jesus Christ. This mindset has also produced lifelong friendships with some of the most interesting people in the world. One of those friends is Dr. Ming Wang. He is a respected laser eye surgeon with a MD (magna cum laude) from Harvard and MIT and a PhD in laser physics. His accomplishments in life are staggering since coming to America from China during Mao's cultural revolution.

On March 7, 2020, while having coffee with Ming in the backyard at his home, he shared his burden with me about the downward spiral he was witnessing in American culture due to what he called a hyper-polarized condition. He told me that he wanted to devote the rest of his life to helping people find common ground in order to combat the plague of polarization. He spoke about this as if he were trying to find the cure for a fatal disease. He looked at me that afternoon and asked me if I would join him in this effort. I instantly accepted his offer.

Though Ming and I are both Christians, we are coming at this problem from different perspectives. Ming is a doctor and scientist whose primary burden is to see the political and socio-economic issues addressed in a civil manner. With that said, he is very bold about his witness for Christ and has spoken at more than two hundred churches in the Middle Tennessee area. I am a pastor, campus minister, and author. I featured Ming's testimony in a book I wrote called *God's Not Dead*, which inspired a movie series by the same name. The inspiration for a character in the movie, a Chinese student named Martin, was Ming's life. For years I have spoken on university campuses in more than forty countries, addressing the issues of faith and skepticism. Ming has joined me for several of these campus presentations. An important part of my mission is to see believers and unbelievers have a better dialogue about these critical issues. This is why the idea of finding common ground resonated with me so strongly. It struck me that this concept was a missing piece in the thinking of most Christians.

For the most part, Christians have developed a somewhat adversarial role with unbelievers. Ironically, many times it takes initiative on the part of a non-Christian to start the dialogue about faith in God in a respectful manner. This is why evangelism is so lacking in most churches and there has been a growing trend of young people exiting the church and ultimately leaving the Christian faith completely. The tragedy is that this exodus didn't have to happen. Not only have believers been ill-equipped to explain the reasons for their faith as 1 Peter 3:15 directs—"Always be prepared to give an answer to everyone who asks you to give the reason for the hope that you have. But do this with gentleness and respect" (NIV)—but there has been a glaring absence of "gentleness and respect." Sharing the truth about what we believe isn't enough; it's also critical that our demeanor be respectful. Finding common ground isn't about abandoning our beliefs; it is about getting rid of the negative, adversarial tone and presentation.

I began to address this very problem directly in 2010, with the introduction of a dialogical tool called "The God Test." It was a simple survey that began with the question "Do you believe in God?" If the person said yes, they would be asked ten more questions. If they said no, they were asked ten different questions. Along with this survey, I introduced a simple teaching called "SALT." SALT is an acronym that stands for start a conversation, ask questions, listen, tell the story. I stressed the importance of asking questions and genuinely listening to others speak. Everyone who has gone through this training has remarked how different the tone of their dialogues with unbelievers has become by utilizing this approach. For the most part, Christians have used what I sarcastically call the TALK method: start talking, argue, get louder, and then kick the unbeliever. Obviously, this is hyperbole, but there is enough truth in this acronym to help us realize how counterproductive many of our efforts have been.

I am not exaggerating when I say that the God Test accompanied by the use of the SALT approach has revolutionized evangelism on campuses around the world. The God Test app has been downloaded in more than 180 countries, and hundreds of thousands of conversations have taken place in a respectful, polite manner. It's not uncommon to have atheists actually thank us for such a refreshingly enjoyable experience. You will discover, along with the thousands that are utilizing the SALT principle, that having dialogues about normally contentious issues is possible. You just need a strategy. Common Ground is the next step in this same direction. By becoming aware of the benefit of finding common ground with others, you will begin to search for it everywhere. Doing so has become almost an obsession for me. In fact, I utilize the SALT principle as one of the primary ways to discover how I might find common ground with others. It doesn't take much to start cultivating a friendship that allows the free exchange of ideas, worldviews, and beliefs without getting into a war like you see on cable news. I will introduce another acronym called STEPS, which I will explain in the coming pages. Hopefully these steps will help remind you of some of the important traits of a common-ground seeker. Common ground is not compromise. It is a method that reduces the annoying background noise that is heard in most of our public dialogue when presenting the gospel.

Our book, *The Common Ground Solution*, goes into greater detail about the key issues of why we are so polarized, what is common ground, and how can we find it with others on the opposite end of the ideological spectrum. This study, however, examines the Scriptures to discover how God expects us to act and speak to others. I once attended a sporting event with a Christian friend and his son. This man was a very respectful, polite person when he was at church. So I was shocked to hear the insults and criticisms coming out of his mouth directed at the referee and the opposing team. I was embarrassed. I wondered what his son was learning about how his father's faith didn't apply at sporting events (unless he prayed for his team to win). This same kind of split personality emerges when believers talk about politicians or other cultural figures they don't agree with. This study is focused on ending this type of bifurcation.

We will examine the character of a person whose words carry influence. Of course, the biblical prophets sometimes spoke difficult things to people. But when people ignore the admonition of gentleness and respect and rush to quote Isaiah or Jeremiah, I remind them that the strong language the prophets used came after years of appeals and tears. It's ironic how believers claim that the harsh judgments in the Old Testament don't apply to their sins because Jesus brought forth a new covenant that they are guided by, yet they want to treat unbelievers as if they are living twenty-five hundred years ago.

Think about it: Would you have come to faith in Christ if you had to overcome Christians shouting at you and insulting you? I bet God used someone who showed you kindness and mercy. Their nonjudgmental tone didn't mean they didn't tell you the truth—they spoke the truth in love. This is my story. If anyone deserved to be insulted for their behavior, it was me. I did things that I'm deeply ashamed of today when I recall my life before I came to know Christ. It was the love of God shown to me through others that caused me to cry out to God for His mercy and see real change come to my heart and mind. I am reminded of Romans 2:4, "God's kindness is intended to lead you to repentance" (NIV).

Repentance is as important as faith. You can learn about this topic more in *The Purple Book*—a similar Bible study that has been translated into twenty-six languages and has almost two million copies in print. Repentance means to change your mind. So make a simple logical connection: If God's kindness leads you to repentance, what will it take to get others to change their minds? The answer is *kindness*!

Over the coming weeks as you go through this study, you will be encouraged to see what the Scriptures say about the importance of believers finding common ground with unbelievers. As you develop this fresh tone in your dialogues and start learning to seek common ground with others, you will see every area of your life affected. You'll find a noticeable improvement in your own mental and emotional health. Noted psychiatrist and mental health expert Dr. Daniel Amen, who has more than ten *New York Times* bestsellers to his credit, is a big fan of the common-ground approach you'll be studying here. Our friendship has centered around improving people's lives by addressing issues surrounding brain health and its impact on the emotions. He said, "If people learn to put the lessons in this book into practice, they will see a dramatic improvement in their own mental hygiene."

We offer this study in hopes that Christian believers of all denominations will gain the right approach to delivering the life-changing message of the gospel in a credible manner. We also hope that this tone and attitude will not be limited to your dialogues about faith but will extend to every other issue you discuss with others.

Introduction:

OUR CALLING TO COMMON GROUND

In this series we will study the traits we are called to possess that make us bridge builders and reconcilers in a polarized world. Possessing these traits will enable us to find common ground with people regardless of their religious, political, or ideological beliefs. For those who believe in God and, more specifically, are followers of Christ, there is a "call to character." The fruit of the Spirit is "love, joy, peace, patience, kindness, goodness, faithfulness, gentleness, self-control" (Galatians 5:22–23). The presence of the Spirit in our lives will produce a work of grace that allows us to exhibit these traits even if we are prone to the opposite. We live in an exciting hour when we can make a great impact on the world by the way we live and treat others. One of the most important truths I learned as a new Christian was that people would know I was a Christian by my actions more than my words. We've all been embarrassed when someone acts unbecomingly and thus discredits the faith they profess.

In this study we will look closely at what the Scriptures say about Christlike character. The "open secret" is that if we are followers of Christ, we are called to be common-ground seekers. This means we find a place of personal connection that allows for a genuine exchange of ideas, thoughts, and ultimately truth. Even if you have truth to tell someone, it won't be of any benefit unless you are in close enough proximity to communicate with them. This is the essence of what it means to find common ground. If you are rude, arrogant, or condescending in your tone, your words of truth will likely be rejected.

The phrase *common ground* isn't specifically used in the Bible, but it is demonstrated from beginning to end. You will repeatedly see the call given to be peacemakers, reconcilers, unifiers, and those who are willing to forgive because we have been forgiven. When Jesus reached out to others while He was in His earthly ministry, He found common ground with those who would have been viewed as enemies. His kind treatment of others was so remarkable that the self-righteously intolerant criticized him as being a "friend of sinners."

One of the most notable examples of Jesus' kind treatment of others is recorded in John 4, where He reached out to a woman from Samaria at a public water well. The woman's name is not given, but she has been referred to as "the woman at the well." Jesus simply asked her for a drink of water. He initiated a dialogue with her by utilizing the fact that all people get thirsty. Finding common ground with others can start with a simple question or request. The woman's response to him started a chain reaction that opened the door for her to ask deeper questions about God and express confusion she had about religion in general.

Jesus had to cross several barriers to communicate with this woman. First, she was a Samaritan. This may mean nothing to you now, but two thousand years ago Jews and Samaritans didn't associate with one another. The racial and ethnic tensions of today pale in comparison to those during Jesus' time on earth. Even more glaring was the gender divide. Men and women didn't have freedom to converse. The woman actually responded to Jesus, "'How is it that you, a Jew, ask for a drink from me, a woman of Samaria?' (For Jews have no dealings with Samaritans.)" (John 4:9).

She eventually left the well and went back into her village to tell people about her experience with Jesus, and "many Samaritans from that town believed in him because of the woman's testimony" (John 4:39). All this took place because Jesus found common ground with someone and began a conversation. And He repeated this pattern with many others. He reached out to Roman soldiers who were despised because of their occupation of the nation of Israel. He did the same with despised tax collectors, immoral people, and those who were mentally and emotionally tormented. Time and time again, He practiced kindness, empathy, and grace. If we truly believe that Jesus is the Son of God, then how can we not follow this example?

He came not only to save us but to partner with us to change the world. That means we are called to follow his example if we want our efforts to be effective and successful. How Christ treated His disciples was revolutionary. He told them He did not come to be served but to serve others. He took the lowliest place to make this point unforgettable. He even washed their feet—a task relegated to the least important in others' eyes. He sent His disciples into the world armed with this love and grace. He told them to love their enemies, turn the other cheek when abused, and not to return evil for evil or insult for insult. At the same time, Jesus' followers were to tell the good news about the kingdom of God and share the message of salvation. They were to give reasons for their faith (yet with gentleness and respect). In doing so, they sought ways to find common ground with others. Saul of Tarsus would have a dramatic encounter with the risen Christ and become a great defender of the faith. He would use his Roman name, Paul, after his personal transformation. This act in itself was evidence that he was eager to do everything possible to find common ground with those who were opposite of his primary cultural identity. In writing to the believers in the Greek city of Corinth, he gave one of the best descriptions of what it means to find common ground.

For though I am free from all, I have made myself a servant to all, that I might win more of them. To the Jews I became as a Jew, in order to win Jews. To those under the law I became as one under the law (though not being myself under the law) that I might win those under the law. To those outside the law I became as one outside the law (not being outside the law of God but under the law of Christ) that I might win those outside the law. To the weak I became weak, that I might win the weak. I have become all things to all people, that by all means I might save some. I do it all for the sake of the gospel, that I may share with them in its blessings.

(1 CORINTHIANS 9:19–23)

By becoming all things to all people, Paul in essence was seeking common ground with them. To insult or condemn them would have alienated them before Paul had a chance to have a genuine dialogue with them. He demonstrated this when he entered the city of Athens, Greece, and engaged with the philosophical and religious leaders in the city. Even though he was from another culture, he sought common ground with them in order to communicate his message. Like Jesus, he went to a place in the city that all citizens shared in common—the public square. This was where dialogues took place about the great issues of the day. Paul had found a statue inscribed to "the unknown god." In their passion for pluralism, the city leaders had not wanted to omit honoring any gods, so they erected a statue to the unknown god. Paul saw this statue as potential common ground that he could have with this group of people who were ethnically, philosophically, and religiously different from him.

WALKING IN CHRIST'S STEPS

In the book *The Common Ground Solution,* we discuss the STEPS for finding common ground with others. This acronym stands for **s**ee, **t**rade places, **e**mpathize, **p**ay the price, and **s**eek. It delineates a methodology gleaned by studying the lives of people who have been effective in finding common ground in the midst of difficult circumstances and against impossible odds. Here's a brief description of each aspect of this process.

See. We have to open our eyes and look. Many times what we need to see is right in front of us but we don't intentionally look. If we refuse to see then it reveals a condition that needs to be treated. I (Ming) have spent a lifetime helping people realize they aren't seeing clearly. When your eyes are opened to see common ground with others it improves your entire life. Finding common ground is essential to having a genuine exchange about life's supreme meaning and purpose. Ultimately, what we should see is others the way God sees them so we can treat them the way He would have us treat them by loving them. We also will be able to see the vast areas we share in common that will build bridges for the message of the gospel to come to their lives.

Trade places speaks of the ability to see the other person's perspective. Other ways of saying this are "Walk in their shoes" and "Seek to understand before seeking to be understood." We all have blind spots. When we are willing to see things from someone else's perspective, things become visible that we might not have seen. Sometimes small details can change an entire narrative.

Empathize. The result of this shift in our perspective produces empathy. No other trait is more valuable in the times we are living in than empathy—feeling someone else's burden or pain. As humans we share in the struggles that life presents. Sickness, death, loss, pain, and heartache will come to us all at some point. Listening to others is indispensable in helping us develop empathy. It gives our words to them greater weight when they believe we sincerely care about them.

Pay the Price. In this process you must be willing to honestly assess your life and recognize any discrimination, racism, polarizing tendencies and be willing to strive to eliminate them. There is a price to pay. Giving up life-long attitudes and stereotypes is difficult. You might have to walk away from people who are determined to remain in a state of anger and outrage—viewing you as an enemy for not sharing their sentiments. It may also mean partnering with people that are wanting to be a peacemaker instead of a polarizer. These partnerships might even be with those you have previously viewed as "those people" or "that group." To make significant change can be costly. The reward, however, is well worth it.

Seek. We are sent out to seek the lost and to help the hurting. We are instructed to "seek first the kingdom of God and his righteousness" (Matthew 6:33). To seek means to diligently search. To seek something earnestly is to make it your top priority. Common-ground seekers are constantly looking for open doors and opportunities to serve others. Living this way turns us from looking inward to looking outward toward others. It is a paradigm shift that yields greater happiness and contentment.

These STEPS are significant because they were modeled by Christ Himself. *He saw* the needs of humanity and our broken condition. Salvation began with His initiation. "God so loved the world, that he gave his only Son" (John 3:16). Salvation isn't a result of humans reaching up to God, but of Him reaching out to us because He saw what we needed.

He traded places. God became man in Christ. Athanasius said, "He became what He was not, without ceasing to be what He was." This means Christ took on flesh without ceasing to be the second person of the Trinity. The Nicene Creed speaks of Christ as "God from God, light from light, true God from true God."

He showed empathy. Christ was moved with compassion and healed those who were sick and helped those who were hurting. His love for us compelled Him to die on the cross in our place. His death paid the penalty for our transgressions and gave us freedom from its cruel grip.

He paid the price. Christ gave His life on a Roman cross to pay the price for our sin and injustice. His sacrifice on our behalf allows us to be forgiven and have a fresh start with God and one another.

He was the seeker. Jesus announced His purpose when He said, "The Son of Man came to seek and to save the lost" (Luke 19:10). He was constantly reaching out to the unreached, unloved, and disenfranchised. He modeled for us what it means to seek common ground with others who are totally different from us.

This study will complement these STEPS by giving you the inward motivation and strength to treat others in a way that honors God. My hope is to examine the Bible closely in these studies and rediscover this ancient calling to be a people who are called Christians because we are imitating Christ. May God help us to be vessels of honor that allow his Spirit to flow through us as we faithfully answer the calling to the ministry of reconciliation. This four-week Bible study is designed to be used in small groups to help you become a common-ground seeker as well as to develop traits that will make you more successful in your relationships.

Lesson 1:

"BLESSED ARE THE PEACEMAKERS"

The most famous discourse in human history was given by Jesus Christ in the region of the Sea of Galilee in Israel and is referred to as the Sermon on the Mount. I lived in Israel a few years ago and spent a lot of time in the area where this message was delivered. The words are timeless and certainly speak to us today. When they were originally given, they were revolutionary. To be meek and merciful was to be relegated to permanent servitude and hardship. Christ offered a view of life that seemed antithetical to conventional wisdom. He was truly describing the road less traveled. His call to those who would follow Him requires a lifestyle far different from that of those who seek power and fame at all costs.

Here is an excerpt from this message.

"Blessed are the poor in spirit,
for theirs is the kingdom of heaven.
"Blessed are those who mourn,
for they shall be comforted.
"Blessed are the meek,
for they shall inherit the earth.
"Blessed are those who hunger and thirst
for righteousness, for they shall be satisfied.
"Blessed are the merciful,
for they shall receive mercy.
"Blessed are the pure in heart,
for they shall see God.
"Blessed are the peacemakers,
for they shall be called
sons of God.

(MATTHEW 5:3–9)

Poor in spirit means to realize how weak and flawed we are. If we think we are superior to others, we become unapproachable and vain in our own self-esteem. Being poor in spirit does not mean we have low self-esteem; it means we don't have an exaggerated sense of self-importance.

To mourn means to care about the pain of others. When we see evil and injustice in the world, we should respond with mercy and empathy. We are further told to rejoice with those who rejoice and to weep with those who weep (Romans 12:15). To weep with others is to show that we share their pain.

To be meek means to be humble. Meekness is not weakness. Living a life of humility takes courage. It means having the desire to listen to others and not be driven by the insecurity of trying to prove someone wrong. This characteristic is so important for common-ground seekers that we will study it more deeply in the next lesson.

To hunger and thirst for righteousness means caring about truth and justice. Seeking common ground doesn't mean we do so at the price of truth. Our hearts should long for a world that is just and fair for all. When we hunger and thirst for something, we make it a top priority.

To be merciful means to give others grace and forgiveness. It is the opposite of being judgmental and critical. As we will see in the next lesson, we are to "love mercy." The opposite of being merciful is to be critical and judgmental. James, the Lord's brother, warned, "Judgment is without mercy to one who has shown no mercy. Mercy triumphs over judgment" (James 2:13).

To be pure in heart is to care about our own sins and weaknesses more than pointing out the sins of others. Jesus said to remove the log from our eye before we try and take the splinter out of our brother's or sister's eye. Those who are pure in heart are prone to seeing the best in people and not the worst. Far from being gullible or naive, being pure in heart keeps us from the deadly cynicism that keeps us from building bridges to others we don't agree with.

To be a peacemaker is to enter every situation with peace as a goal. This doesn't mean "peace at all costs," but it does mean that peace will cost everyone something. We all have to be willing to see things that we can change in order to truly give peace a chance. To be a peacemaker is to be a common-ground seeker. Let's look closer at what else the Scripture says about this.

BECOMING A PEACEMAKER

I had to learn how to be a peacemaker when I became a father. Raising five children produced endless opportunities for conflicts, quarrels, and impasses. My job was not to take sides but to bring resolve while teaching my children to resolve their own quarrels in a righteous manner. Progress was slow—sometimes it seemed they were losing ground and in danger of creating permanent wounds and hurts. Regardless of the circumstances, I knew I couldn't quit trying. I've tried to live with this same kind of commitment in engaging with people as a Christian minister. The lessons I learned as a father have certainly helped with the multitude of situations I have faced. When we think about the prospect of finding common ground with others, there is definitely a universal need for someone to help mediate the multitude of conflicts that arise.

Jesus, the Prince of Peace, said that peacemakers would be blessed. The angels spoke of the peace He would bring when they announced His birth to the shepherds in the fields of Israel (Luke 2:14). Jesus spoke peace to the storms threatening His disciples on the Sea of Galilee (Mark 4:39), and He spoke peace to the storms in the hearts and minds of those who heard Him speak. The call to be a peacemaker is a daunting challenge. Taking sides is much easier. One of the most chilling statements in Scripture is the one that describes what God "hates." On that list are those who "sow discord among brothers" (Proverbs 6:19). He loves unity. Psalm 133:1–3 says, "Behold, how good and pleasant it is when brothers dwell in unity! ... For there the Lord has commanded the blessing, life forevermore."

On the day of Pentecost, after Jesus' resurrection and ascension, He poured out His Holy Spirit upon His followers. The Scripture said the disciples were gathered in an upper room in one accord. They weren't just together; they were together together. This is simple to understand: people in an elevator might be together, but they aren't really together in the sense of being unified and in relationship with one another—unlike the believers in Jesus' day. But the type of unity Jesus' followers had on the day of Pentecost did not come easily. The disciples often argued, accused one another, and turned on each other. All of them abandoned the Lord in His darkest hour. But after His resurrection, Jesus sought them out and restored their relationship with Him and with one another.

SUMMARY

Common-ground seekers are peacemakers. Peace is not a last resort but a primary goal for us with others. Whether in a work situation, a political debate, a relational breach, or an ideological conflict, having the mindset of a peacemaker is an indispensable trait for those desiring to create a better life for themselves and others. This doesn't mean we have a "peace at any cost" mentality, but it does mean that achieving peace will cost everyone something. This is a key aspect necessary in finding common ground.

1. What are we called to seek?

_____

"So then let us pursue what makes for
peace and for mutual upbuilding."
(ROMANS 14:19)

2. Who will gain an inheritance and
have abundant peace?

_____

"The meek shall inherit the land and delight
themselves in abundant peace."
(PSALM 37:11)

3. What is the promise for the person of peace?

_____

"Mark the blameless and behold the upright,
for there is a future for the man of peace."
(PSALM 37:37)

4. Paul described the crisis of the human condition. Besides the poison emanating from the mouths of humans, what is said about their ability to find peace with others?

"Their throat is an open grave;
    they use their tongues to deceive."
"The venom of asps is under their lips."
    "Their mouth is full of curses and bitterness."
"Their feet are swift to shed blood;
    in their paths are ruin and misery,
and the way of peace they have not known."
(ROMANS 3:13–17)

5. What is the gospel called?

"As shoes for your feet... put on the readiness given by the gospel of peace."
(EPHESIANS 6:15)

6. If we truly love life and want to see good days, what are we called to do?

_____

Whoever desires to love life
    and see good days,
let him keep his tongue from evil
    and his lips from speaking deceit;
let him turn away from evil and do good;
    let him seek peace and pursue it.
(1 PETER 3:10–11)

7. Compare the wisdom from above and the wisdom that is destructive. What is promised to those who seek to be peacemakers?

_____

"If you have bitter jealousy and selfish ambition in your hearts, do not boast and be false to the truth. This is not the wisdom that comes down from above, but is earthly, unspiritual, demonic. For where jealousy and selfish ambition exist, there will be disorder and every vile practice. But the wisdom from above is first pure, then peaceable, gentle, open to reason, full of mercy and good fruits, impartial and sincere. And a harvest of righteousness is sown in peace by those who make peace."
(JAMES 3:14–18)

ADDITIONAL LIGHT

"Turn away from evil and do good;
seek peace and pursue it."
(PSALM 34:14)

"How good and pleasant it is when God's people
live together in unity!... For there the Lord bestows
his blessing, even life forevermore."
(PSALM 133:1, 3B NIV)

"Do nothing out of selfish ambition or vain conceit. Rather,
in humility value others above yourselves, not looking to your
own interests but each of you to the interests of the others."
(PHILIPPIANS 2:3-4 NIV)

"Make every effort to keep the unity of the Spirit
through the bond of peace."
(EPHESIANS 4:3 NIV)

"For he himself is our peace, who has made the two groups one
and has destroyed the barrier, the dividing wall of hostility."
(EPHESIANS 2:14 NIV)

"And a harvest of righteousness is sown
in peace by those who make peace."
(JAMES 3:18)

"If it is possible, as far as it depends on you,
live at peace with everyone."
(ROMANS 12:18)

REFLECTIONS

1. Do you think enough emphasis has been placed on the need for Christians to follow the lessons taught by Christ in the Sermon on the Mount?

2. How would the attitude of unbelievers be altered if more Christians lived by the principles taught in the Sermon on the Mount?

3. What is your attitude toward the central thesis of this study that we are to seek common ground with others?

4. How does this alter the way you treat those whom you don't agree with (politically, spiritually, etc.)?

NOTES

NOTES

NOTES

NOTES

Lesson 2:

"DO JUSTICE, LOVE MERCY, WALK HUMBLY"

No better description has been given of the kind of people we are to be as followers of Christ than the one given by the prophet Micah more than twenty-eight hundred years ago.

He has told you, O man, what is good;
and what does the Lord require of you
but to do justice, and to love kindness,
and to walk humbly with your God?

(MICAH 6:8)

To grasp the significance of these words, we need to look at the context of when these words were spoken. The nation of Israel had experienced its greatest unity and peace under the leadership of King Solomon. No other nation had the wealth and power they possessed during this time. This prosperity started under the reign of Solomon's father, King David, and expanded under Solomon. After Solomon's death, his son Rehoboam came to power. The people came to Rehoboam and requested that he lead differently than his father had. They said, "Your father made our yoke heavy. Now therefore, lighten the hard service of your father and his heavy yoke on us, and we will serve you" (1 Kings 12:4). This sounds like a reasonable request. The new king told the people he would consider their request.

He conferred with the older members of the nation who had stood by his Father's side during the unprecedented years of prosperity, and they counseled him, "If you will be a servant to this people today and serve them, and speak good words to them when you answer them, then they will be your servants forever" (12:7).

These wise leaders were giving Rehoboam a priceless gift of wisdom. Serve the people, and they will serve you. But the young king didn't like the notion of being the people's servant. Historically, most leaders have sought power through strength and even intimidation. Rehoboam consulted the younger men, and they gave him an entirely different speech for the people. They said, "Thus shall you speak to this people who said to you, 'Your father made our yoke heavy, but you lighten it for us,' thus shall you say to them, 'My little finger is thicker than my father's thighs. And now, whereas my father laid on you a heavy yoke, I will add to your yoke. My father disciplined you with whips, but I will discipline you with scorpions'" (12:10–11).

The king decided to listen to the advice of the younger leaders and repeated this harsh response to the people of Israel. The results were catastrophic. The national unity came to an end. The nation became polarized, the northern kingdom with a king named Jeroboam and the southern kingdom of Judah led by Rehoboam. This polarization weakened the nation and made it vulnerable to their enemies. Like sharks smelling blood, their adversaries circled them, waiting to take them captive.

After two centuries of this polarization and division, the prophet Micah entered this cultural milieu to try and steer the people back to unity and to a place of peace and protection. If they would have heeded the prophet's words, they would have been spared the calamitous fate that befell both parts of the divided nation. This was certainly an emphasis of Christ. He taught his disciples repeatedly that to be great leaders, they had to be servants.

> *You know that the rulers of the Gentiles*
> *lord it over them, and their great ones*
> *exercise authority over them. It shall not*
> *be so among you. But whoever would be*
> *great among you must be your servant, and*
> *whoever would be first among you must*
> *be your slave, even as the Son of Man*
> *came not to be served but to serve, and to*
> *give his life as a ransom for many.*

(MATTHEW 20:25–28)

This is a lesson for us to hear today. We will look at the three dimensions of this mandate given by the prophet Micah. You don't have to use the words *common ground* to find it with others. As you do justice, love mercy, and walk humbly before your God, you will find yourself surrounded by people who are drawn to the grace on your life and are open to hear what you have to say.

SUMMARY

The calling to do justice, love mercy, and walk humbly is a pattern that will cause us to be effective in all aspects of life. Those who desire to find common ground will discover how others will value these traits when they see them demonstrated through their lives. As followers of Christ, we want to do all that we can to put ourselves in a position to reach out to others and help them discover the love and grace of God. Many times it's our behavior that becomes a stumbling block to others grasping the truth of the Christian faith. Following this mandate from the prophet Micah can make an enormous difference in removing that stumbling block.

"DO JUSTICE"

This means we are to act justly. When people witness injustice, they take to the streets to vent their outrage. Sadly, those who are outraged by injustice sometimes end up acting unjustly in response because not exacting evil for evil takes enormous restraint. Common-ground seekers care about justice, and bringing it about starts with each person determining to walk justly. Regardless of what others do, you must determine to be true to your commitment to God and His Word.

Dr. Martin Luther King Jr. was a true common-ground visionary. He confronted the injustice of racism and discrimination in America with a relentless combination of justice, mercy, and humility. Paraphrasing nineteenth-century abolitionist preacher Theodore Parker, King often remarked, "The moral arc of the universe is long, but it bends toward justice." This moral arc represents God's truth, which is written on every heart. Beyond societal norms there are higher laws that we are to follow. When we truly desire what is right and are not simply concerned about our self-interest, we have a great opportunity to find common ground with others.

1. What did the psalmist say the Lord loves?

_____

"The Lord loves justice; he will
not forsake his saints."
(PSALM 37:28)

2. What did the prophet Amos say the Lord desires more than religious celebrations and solemn assemblies?

_____

"Let justice roll down like waters,
and righteousness like an
ever-flowing stream."
(AMOS 5:24)

3. What did Jesus come to proclaim?

Behold, my servant whom I have chosen,
> my beloved with whom my soul is well pleased.
I will put my Spirit upon him,
> and he will proclaim *justice* to the Gentiles.
He will not quarrel or cry aloud,
> nor will anyone hear his voice in the streets;
a bruised reed he will not break,
> and a smoldering wick he will not quench,
until he brings *justice* to victory;
> and in his name the Gentiles will hope.
(MATTHEW 12:18, EMPHASIS ADDED)

"LOVE MERCY"

Those who seek for justice have a tendency to become unmerciful in this pursuit. We are called to love mercy. Justice is defined as someone getting what they deserve in terms of judgment for their crimes. Receiving mercy means we don't get what we deserve. As common-ground seekers, we are not called to begrudgingly give others mercy—we are to *love* mercy. When we love mercy, we practically overlook insults and attitudes that normally result in broken relationships remaining broken. Those who love mercy are quick to forgive others.

God is merciful. Scripture repeatedly says, "His mercy endures forever." One of the most encouraging passages of Scripture to me is Psalm 103:8–10: "The Lord is merciful and gracious, slow to anger and abounding in steadfast love. He will not always chide, nor will he keep his anger forever. He does not deal with us according to our sins, nor repay us according to our iniquities."

God does not treat us as our sins deserve. If God treats us this way, how much more should we treat others the same way? To actually love mercy means we look for the smallest reason to extend it to others. When we have this mindset, we will continually reach out to others from whom we would otherwise remain alienated.

4. **What is the cry of the psalmist?**

_____

"Have mercy upon us, O Lord, have mercy upon us, for we have had more than enough of contempt."
(PSALM 123:3)

5. **What did Jesus tell the unmerciful leaders that they needed to learn?**

_____

"Go and learn what this means: 'I desire mercy, and not sacrifice.' For I came not to call the righteous, but sinners."
(MATTHEW 9:13)

6. If we show no mercy, what will judgment be like for us?

_____

"For judgment is without mercy to one who has shown no mercy. Mercy triumphs over judgment."

(JAMES 2:13)

"WALK HUMBLY"

Humility is becoming a scarce commodity. In an age of indulgent self-promotion on social media, it's becoming more and more likely to hear someone's accomplishments than their struggles. We don't expect people to show us an unflattering selfie. Humility is not thinking less of yourself; it's thinking of yourself less. When you hear athletes giving the credit to their teammates instead of taking the credit, you are hearing humility. When someone succeeds in any endeavor in life and sincerely expresses gratitude for everyone who has helped them along the way, you are witnessing humility. Walking in humility means seeing the value in every human being regardless of their ethnicity or economic status.

Having this kind of attitude causes you to be seen as a person who can be trusted. In the midst of any conflict, maintaining an attitude of humility gives you the greatest chance for a resolution. The Bible says, "God opposes the proud, but gives grace to the humble" (James 4:6). If God opposes the proud, people will oppose you as well. Walking humbly gives you the best chance for others to consider your opinion or point of view. We cultivate humility by respecting others, listening to them speak without interruption, and recognizing that they might be saying something that we should consider. Whether the issue is a difference in opinion about politics, sports, or social turmoil, walking humbly will set you apart and give you the greatest chance to make a difference.

7. **What will happen to those who humble themselves?**

_____

"Everyone who exalts himself will be humbled,
and he who humbles himself will be exalted."
(LUKE 14:11)

8. **What happens to those who walk in pride?**

_____

"When pride comes, then comes disgrace,
but with the humble is wisdom."
(PROVERBS 11:2)

9. Describe the type of mind we are called to have.

_____

"All of you, have unity of mind, sympathy, brotherly love,
a tender heart, and a humble mind."
(1 PETER 3:8)

10. How did the apostle Paul act as a leader
in the presence of those he led?

_____

"I, Paul, myself entreat you, by the meekness and gentleness
of Christ—I who am humble when face to face with you,
but bold toward you when I am away!"
(2 CORINTHIANS 10:1)

ADDITIONAL LIGHT

"The LORD detests dishonest scales,
but accurate weights find favor with him."
(PROVERBS 11:1 NIV)

"The wicked accepts a bribe in secret
to pervert the ways of justice."
(PROVERBS 17:23)

"Open your mouth for the mute, for the rights of all
who are destitute. Open your mouth, judge righteously,
defend the rights of the poor and needy."
(PROVERBS 31:8-9)

"Abhor what is evil; hold fast to what is good."
(ROMANS 12:9)

"Let each of you look not only to his own interests,
but also to the interests of others."
(PHILIPPIANS 2:4)

"Do not repay anyone evil for evil. Be careful to do
what is right in the eyes of everyone."
(ROMANS 12:17)

"Therefore, as God's chosen people, holy and
dearly loved, clothe yourselves with compassion,
kindness, humility, gentleness and patience."
(COLOSSIANS 3:12)

REFLECTIONS

1. How can you seek for justice while being merciful?

2. Doing justice starts with us as individuals. How can we avoid the hypocrisy of seeking to call out injustice in others before dealing with ourselves first?

3. What are the areas of injustice that need to be addressed in your community?

4. Who are other people you know who share the same call to reach out and address these areas of need?

NOTES

NOTES

NOTES

NOTES

Lesson 3:

THE WAY OF WISDOM

When it comes to finding common ground with others, no attribute is more valuable than wisdom. We are told in Scripture to value wisdom more than silver or gold. It's to be desired more than anything else. And yet wisdom is difficult to define because it is so broad and all-encompassing in the areas it affects. Wisdom involves knowledge, but it's more than that. A typical dictionary definition is that wisdom is the quality of having experience, knowledge, and good judgment. Wisdom is the ability to apply knowledge in a way that results in productivity, growth, and success in every area of life. That's why there's a distinction between being smart and being wise. We certainly want to study and be knowledgeable about what we are talking about, but wisdom will help make your knowledge more acceptable to your listeners. In the book of Proverbs, wisdom is personified and speaks of its companions: "I, wisdom, dwell with prudence, and I find knowledge and discretion" (Proverbs 8:12).

I call these words the "forgotten words of Proverbs." You rarely hear words like *prudence* and *discretion* being used in the average conversation. *Prudence* means conducting yourself with reason and common sense. *Discretion* means knowing what to say at the appropriate time. Someone lacking discretion may be knowledgeable but say things at the wrong time or in a way that comes across as rude and insensitive. Good medical doctors know the importance of speaking to their patients with wisdom and discretion. Dr. Ming Wang stresses to his staff, "Speak in the language of the listener." He means to use as little technical language as possible and to help them understand their condition in as hopeful a manner as possible. For those who are committed to the advancement of the gospel, possessing wisdom (and all its companions) is indispensable.

The more we reach out to others, the more we will put a premium on wisdom. The Christian faith has been marginalized by those who think they are being bold when in reality they are just being obnoxious. This may sound harsh, but it's true. More than once, while traveling by air, I have overheard a Christian loudly share his or her faith with a fellow passenger and have wanted to apologize to those on board for being subjected to the discourteous behavior.

Early in my Christian life, I heard a message based on this verse from the book of Proverbs: "The fruit of the righteous is a tree of life, and *he who wins souls is wise*" (11:30 NKJV, emphasis added).

This is an important truth to ponder deeply. If you truly desire to win hearts and minds for Christ, then becoming a person of wisdom should be a passion. The primary reason wisdom is a necessity is because of the complexity of people's beliefs. Some will state that they have strictly rational or logic reasons for rejecting the Christian faith when in fact they actually have deeply emotional motivations. Helping them discover this truth isn't easy. It takes a person of wisdom to ask questions, listen carefully, and help people evaluate and reconsider their fundamental beliefs.

One of the legendary figures of history, Socrates, employed this methodology. We learn of him through the writings of his disciple Plato. Socrates would ask people questions and help them discover the limits of their knowledge. Asking questions remains a powerful tool for those desiring to walk in the way of wisdom. Inviting others to explore and share their thoughts causes them to be more open to what you have to say. To be an effective witness for Christ, you must walk in wisdom. The apostle Paul implored his fellow believers not just to communicate the gospel faithfully, but to do it in a fashion that honored God. Every person is unique. They deserve to hear the truth in a way that specifically addresses their situation.

Paul admonished believers, "Be wise in the way you act toward outsiders; make the most of every opportunity. Let your conversation be always full of grace, seasoned with salt, so that you may know how to answer everyone" (Colossians 4:5–6 NIV). "Outsiders" refers to those outside of the Christian faith. The opportunities Paul referred to are the circumstances in which you suddenly become aware of the common ground you have to share with others. Sometimes it's an unexpected encounter. We are told to walk in wisdom in these moments. In other cases, your opportunity might be the result of a strategic insight that allows you to find common ground with others. Sometimes the scope of the common ground is so small it can be dismissed or ignored.

Wisdom will help you see how valuable this small piece of common ground really is and to fan the flame of what appears to be a smoldering wick. The wrong word at a delicate time can extinguish that small flicker of hope. That's why we cannot overstate the fact that people who are wise are recognized not just by the words they speak but the way they speak.

We must learn how to be wise—it doesn't come naturally. Human nature causes us to act in ways that for the most part are antithetical to the way of wisdom. Some of the words used to describe those who are unwise are *proud, foolish, scorner, scoffer,* and *unrighteous.* Scripture predicts the fate of those who behave in these unbecoming ways, saying they will come to dishonor and ruin. On the other hand, the character of the wise causes them to be successful regardless of their economic status, education, or ethnic background. Wisdom is available to everyone who asks for it earnestly and seeks for it diligently. "If any of you lacks wisdom, let him ask God, who gives generously to all without reproach, and it will be given him" (James 1:5).

What is ironic is how much Scripture speaks about our need to seek wisdom and how freely God will give it yet how allusive it seems to be for so many. Pursuing wisdom must become a top priority in terms of our prayer life. This was certainly the case for Jesus' original disciples. They were considered uneducated and untrained men and women. The majority of them had a low social standing. Christ consistently chose the lowly, the least, and the last in terms of those the culture would esteem. God calls people based on His grace, not according to their natural talents and abilities. This should give us all hope. That doesn't mean we dismiss education. We are to study and learn the reasons our faith is valid. The reality is that when we engage others with the gospel, it doesn't come down to arguments and debate.

Sometimes an "aha" moment of insight makes all the experiences and knowledge someone has had come together to change their minds and embrace the gospel. Wisdom will give us insight into the key issues and obstacles with which those we speak are struggling so that we can facilitate that moment of enlightenment. And in times when we face fierce reactions to our message, we can claim Christ's promise to give us supernatural wisdom to help us in times when we face opposition: "I will give you a mouth and wisdom, which none of your adversaries will be able to withstand or contradict" (Luke 21:15).

Walking the way of wisdom requires effort and diligence. We have to search for wisdom diligently, ask for it in faith, and desire it more than anything else. If we commit ourselves to this pursuit of wisdom, we can have confidence that it will make an impact on the lives we are hoping to reach for Christ. Failing to have wisdom perpetuates a broken and ineffective witness. The stories of those who walk in wisdom should inspire us not to settle for meager results in evangelism. Finding common ground is the result of wisdom. When you speak humbly and graciously, people will lower their defenses and open their hearts and minds to hear what you have to say, and you will find doors opening.

Perhaps the greatest motivation is the reality that people's eternal destinies are at stake. Failing to be wise could result in becoming a stumbling block to someone struggling to find faith in God. That's why the prophet Daniel spoke of the blessing that awaits persons of wisdom and those who engage others in evangelism. Written over five hundred years before the time of Christ, his words foretell the eternal significance of our actions in this life. "Many of those who sleep in the dust of the earth shall awake, some to everlasting life, and some to shame and everlasting contempt. And those who are wise shall shine like the brightness of the sky above; and those who turn many to righteousness, like the stars forever and ever" (Daniel 12:2–3).

With this in mind, let's study other traits that mark the way of wisdom. These verses should help us grasp the truth that how we say something is just as important as what we say.

SUMMARY

Possessing wisdom is necessary for being an effective witness and ambassador for Christ. Godly wisdom is available to anyone who asks and seeks for it diligently. It will produce graciousness in your speech and give you discretion to know what to say and when to say it. It will also cause you to seek common ground with others and value it, regardless of how small or insignificant it may seem. If modern physics has taught us anything, great power resides in small packages. Wisdom will help us unlock this power to transform negative situations into positive ones, and moreover, it will transform people's lives so that they are no longer walking in darkness but in the light of Christ. This is our greatest mission as Christ's followers.

THE MARKS OF WISDOM

Many dimensions and character traits are involved in the life of wisdom. Here are a few of those traits that are indispensable for those who will be viewed as wise.

ONE WHO LISTENS

A key trait of the way of wisdom that helps you find common ground is the habit of listening. It's becoming a lost art. We can learn so much more when we're listening and not talking.

1. **What is said of a person who speaks before they listen?**

_____

"If one gives an answer before he hears,
it is his folly and shame."
(PROVERBS 18:13)

2. **How will others view you if you are slow to speak?**

_____

"Whoever restrains his words has knowledge,
and he who has a cool spirit is a man
of understanding. Even a fool who keeps silent
is considered wise; when he closes his lips,
he is deemed intelligent."
(PROVERBS 17:27–28)

I've been challenged by these verses for years. When a difficult dialogue happens and something is said that I strongly disagree with, I've let my vexation be known immediately. I've had to work hard to resist this tendency.

3. **James, the Lord's brother, said we are to be quick to hear, slow to speak, and**

_____

"Let every person be quick to hear, slow to speak, slow to anger; for the anger of man does not produce the righteousness of God."
(JAMES 1:19–20)

4. **This kind of unrighteous anger stirs up strife and**

_____

"A man of wrath stirs up strife, and one given to anger causes much transgression."
(PROVERBS 29:22)

NOT QUARRELSOME

Anger invariably produces quarrels. In our current cultural climate, "quarrel" sounds mild. Very little comes out of a verbal battle, so we are considered wise for avoiding quarrels. On the other hand, those who consistently find themselves in such exchanges are counted as foolish.

5. **Paul strongly instructed Timothy not to be**

_____

"The Lord's servant must not be quarrelsome
but kind to everyone, able to teach, patiently
enduring evil, correcting his opponents
with gentleness."
(2 TIMOTHY 2:24–25)

6. **What are told to do if we sense a quarrel breaking out?**

_____

"The beginning of strife is like letting out water,
so quit before the quarrel breaks out."
(PROVERBS 17:14)

SPEAKS GRACIOUSLY

The grace God granted us in salvation is the kind of grace we should extend to others. Every person is made in the image of God and should be treated as such. But because that isn't always easy to do, we need to pray and ask for God's Spirit to give us this ability. We must speak graciously to be effective ambassadors for Christ.

7. **How are we told our speech is to be at all times?**

_____

"Let your speech always be gracious, seasoned with salt,
so that you may know how you ought to
answer each person."
(COLOSSIANS 4:6)

8. **What is the promise for those whose speech is gracious?**

_____

"He who loves purity of heart, and whose speech
is gracious, will have the king as his friend."
(PROVERBS 22:11)

ADDITIONAL LIGHT

*"The purpose in a man's heart is like deep water, but
a man of understanding will draw it out."*
(PROVERBS 20:5)

*"The way of a fool is right in his own eyes, but a wise man
listens to advice. The vexation of a fool is known at once,
but the prudent ignores an insult."*
(PROVERBS 12:15–16)

*"Scoffers set a city aflame, but the wise turn away wrath.
If a wise man has an argument with a fool,
the fool only rages and laughs, and there is no quiet."*
(PROVERBS 29:8–9)

*"Whoever is slow to anger is better than the mighty, and
he who rules his spirit than he who takes a city."*
(PROVERBS 16:32)

*"A soft answer turns away wrath, but a
harsh word stirs up anger."*
(PROVERBS 15:1)

REFLECTIONS

1. How does this lesson change your
   perspective on evangelism?

2. What is the impact of the cause of Christ
   when people fail to use wisdom
   in their Christian witness?

3. How can wisdom impact the search for
   common ground with others?

NOTES

NOTES

NOTES

NOTES

Lesson 4:

SEEKING COMMON GROUND

Now we come to the place of stepping out and seeking to build bridges with others. Our calling as believers is to take the gospel (good news) of Jesus Christ to all nations. This requires that we engage with people and build relationships that can lead to life-changing conversations. Our motivation is more than just wanting someone to follow Jesus; it's to demonstrate Christ's love for them through our lives. The love of God should motivate us to help as many people as possible.

Taking the gospel to all nations doesn't mean you have to travel to a foreign country. The world has come to us. In cities like Nashville where Ming and I live, people of more than 130 nationalities reside. We have an unprecedented opportunity to reach the world by simply crossing the street. Scripture says that we are to show "hospitality" (Hebrews 13:2; 1 Peter 4:9). This word literally means "to be a friend of the foreigner."

We live in a polarized, broken world. This brokenness affects our ability to communicate with one another, especially if we are from different "tribes"—not just people of different ethnicities, but political, economic, and social tribes as well. Our tendency to form tribes is not wrong. It's just what we do as humans. We can form them around just about anything, from a sports team to a motorcycle club. The problem comes when differences turn into tribal warfare. This is our sad condition today. America hasn't been this divided since the Civil War. Our polarization has metastasized into a cancerous condition that turns the opposing side into an evil enemy. The power of social media has driven this division into chasms that separate us in an unprecedented way. We must be motivated by Christ's calling and God's love to overcome these barriers. As believers, do we really have any other choice?

Simply put, when we seek to find common ground with others, we are intentionally attempting to build bridges across these great divides. In this lesson, we will look briefly at a methodology for finding common ground that was gleaned from the lives of people currently involved in this noble effort as well as those who have practiced it throughout history. We will use the acronym STEPS as a mnemonic tool to help you remember the steps to finding common ground. First, however, let's go over a few basic things to keep in mind as we launch out into these troubled waters. Here are key truths to remember:

THE GOSPEL

As a believer, this is your primary message to give to the world. Scripture says, "For God so loved the world, that he gave his only Son, that whoever believes in him should not perish but have eternal life" (John 3:16).

Jesus came into a broken, hostile world and loved those who considered Him their enemy. He told His disciples that they were to "love their enemies" as well. This was a revolutionary concept. When we find common ground with others, we create a place where each side's beliefs can be openly and honestly shared. Because the gospel is true—that is, based on historical facts (Christ's life, death and resurrection)—we can have confidence in its power to stand up under the weight of skeptical scrutiny. There are many tools you can access to help you answer questions that arise when you present the gospel.

Here is a basic definition of the gospel
that you should know:

*The gospel is the good news that God became man
in Jesus Christ; He lived the life we should have lived, and
He died the death we should have died—in our place.
Three days later He rose again from the dead,
proving He is the Son of God and offering the gift
of salvation and the forgiveness of sins to
everyone who repents and believes in Him.*

The key thing to remember is that Christ was crucified in history. It really happened. You could know this historical fact apart from the Bible. His tomb was found empty three days after

His crucifixion by a group of His women followers. This, too, is a historical fact. Christianity started three days after Jesus' public death on a Roman cross. History records that these early followers claimed that Jesus appeared to them. Skeptics concede this but are quick to demure that this must have been a mass hallucination. Psychologists tell us that hallucinations don't happen en masse. More than five hundred witnesses saw Jesus alive. History also tells us that seven of the twelve original disciples died a martyr's death rather than deny Jesus' resurrection. Many people die for what they believe to be true, but no one dies for what they know to be false. They knew He had been raised from the dead. This fact is critical, because the truth of the Christian faith rests on this historical event—Christ's resurrection from the dead. As Paul wrote,

> *"If Christ has not been raised, your faith is futile and you are still in your sins."*
>
> (1 CORINTHIANS 15:17)

THE GOSPEL INCLUDES SOCIAL JUSTICE

Recall lesson 2, "Do Justice, Love Mercy, Walk Humbly." We don't choose between the gospel and social justice issues. In fact, the great social issues of our day give us common ground with people who are burdened by these things. We as believers should be grieved at injustice in society and moved to action. When crisis happens in the culture, we should be the first on the scene to help. We don't come to take sides but to seek justice and peace. Many times those who want justice don't like mercy. But we are to love mercy! We are called into the storms that rage in our cities and nations. Some of the greatest times of spiritual awakening have come in the midst of potential revolutions.

It comes down to the voices present or absent at the table. To fail to care or show empathy is to surrender our calling as followers of Christ. To fall into the trap of looking at the crisis through a political or ideological narrative is to abandon the Christian worldview. We are to be people who care about truth, for it's the truth that sets people free. We must carry ourselves as peacemakers and reconcilers if we are to make a difference and see change. We must be willing to listen to others first if we want to be heard ourselves.

The gospel is the ultimate human rights issue. When an outcry occurs over some kind of evil taking place, people look for answers. How can we stop the cycle of violence and injustice? Laws can only do so much. The legal system is woefully inadequate to fix society. The answer lies in the need for human hearts to change. The gospel deals with the source of injustice— the human heart. When our hearts are transformed, our actions will follow.

THE MINISTRY OF RECONCILIATION

If you are a follower of Christ, you are called to the ministry of reconciliation.

You and I were reconciled to God through the death of Christ. Our response to this gracious gift is to be willing to help others be reconciled as well. The good news, the gospel, is that Christ paid the price for our sins, and this is a remarkable, life-changing reality.

If anyone is in Christ, he is a new creation.
The old has passed away; behold, the new has come.
All this is from God, who through Christ reconciled us to
himself and gave us the ministry of reconciliation; that is,
in Christ God was reconciling the world to himself,
not counting their trespasses against them, and entrusting
to us the message of reconciliation. Therefore, we are
ambassadors for Christ, God making his appeal through us.
We implore you on behalf of Christ, be reconciled to God.

(2 Corinthians 5:17–20)

Reconciliation is not just about us being reconciled to God, but about being reconciled to one another too. In the Lord's Prayer, we ask to be forgiven as we forgive those who sin against us. In fact, one of Jesus' most chilling statements is "If you do not forgive others their trespasses, neither will your Father forgive your trespasses" (Matthew 6:15). When I think of these words, they produce "the fear of the Lord" in me, and as Scripture says, "The fear of the Lord is the beginning of wisdom" (Proverbs 9:10).

Fear is like cholesterol: there are two kinds, good and bad. The fear of the Lord is the good kind of fear that motivates us to choose good and not evil. Regardless of whether "I feel like forgiving," the knowledge that forgiveness of my own sins is connected to my willingness to forgive others makes the right choice a "no brainer."

CONNECTION NOT COMPROMISE

Finding common ground with others is about making a relational connection that can lead to a genuine dialogue about any issue—it doesn't mean we compromise our beliefs or convictions. We are really talking about adding to our convictions, not subtracting. We should hold these truths we have examined in this study just as firmly as any other conviction. I can't dismiss being a peacemaker or walking humbly in the name of my "righteous anger."

Rarely have I had to resort to hostility with someone in any potential conflict. As we learned in lesson 3, we can walk away from this type of dialogue before it turns into something negative. Doing so is certainly not easy. It requires a lot of prayer and grace. I've failed to live up to this standard more times than I can count, but over time and with patience and determination, I've learned that we can develop these habits that help us find common ground with others.

Some things you might consider to be convictions might be changed in this process. In the past, I considered a lot of things to be fundamental to my faith that I shouldn't have held in such high regard. We sometimes make our tribal traditions equal to the commands of Scripture. I'm reminded of the dispute described in Acts 15 over the practice of circumcision. One faction believed circumcision was necessary for salvation. The church leaders met in Jerusalem to discuss the issue and determined that the practice was not essential. The people who held circumcision as a conviction needed courage to be willing to give up their tradition when they were confronted with the truth. We should remember the words of Peter Medeirlin, a German Lutheran pastor, from the seventeenth century: "In the essentials, unity, in the non-essentials liberty, and in all things charity."

STEPS TO COMMON GROUND

We now come to the methodology for finding common ground. Dr. Wang has stressed the importance of providing a process that can be applied to any issue, conflict, or area of need. I am grateful to partner with a medical doctor and scientist in this endeavor. We have looked at Scripture as well as at the lives of those who have practiced this methodology. As we wrote down the "best practices" we extracted, we saw these principles crystalizing in the acronym STEPS. We expand on this acronym in the book *The Common Ground Solution* but provide an overview here for those with a passion to begin building common ground with others.

SEE

Open your eyes. In order to see clearly, we must have any obstructions removed from our sight and be willing to deal with the personal issues that make us unwilling to see what is right before us. Many things can be right in front of us and we miss them. Our vision is priceless. If we refuse to see then it reveals a condition that needs to be treated. Ming and I have spent a lifetime helping people to see more clearly—both physically and spiritually. The good news is that if you are reading these words, you are demonstrating your desire for expanded vision. This is the starting point in the common ground seeking process. As a believer, you should be motivated by the command of Jesus to *"go therefore and make disciples of all nations"* (Matthew 28:19).

Looking for common ground with others is indispensable if you are trying to share the gospel. You must be close enough to have a conversation remembering that a dialogue goes in two directions—you have to listen as well as talk.

Finding common ground can take place in countless ways. Human need is everywhere. For instance, Dr. Wang is deeply burdened by the political polarization that exists in America. He wants to see this gridlock and strife treated like a virus and eliminated. Not all common-ground encounters and initiatives will result in a gospel conversation. Your faith, however, will make a lasting impression as you demonstrate the fruit of the Spirit in your life.

TRADE PLACES

Trading places is a skill that can produce a true change in perspective toward a person or group of people that you have written off as evil. Of course, there are extreme hate groups that are never going to listen to you or should not even be approached. Outside of those exceptions, the majority of situations afford an opportunity to build a bridge to others or break down a barrier. We all know the expression "Walk a mile in someone else's shoes." This is the essence of trading places. As a pastor, I am constantly telling people to reach out to people of a different ethnicity. It's amazing what you will learn when you travel and experience other cultures. Minimally, we should be people who master this technique of seeing life from another perspective.

EMPATHIZE

Showing empathy is at the heart of what it means to be a follower of Christ. Philosopher Esther Lightcap Meek, in her book *A Little Manual for Knowing,* says, "To show empathy is to demonstrate you understand the feelings and concerns of others, empathetically putting yourself inside the thing you want to know, and taking it inside you."

As I have spoken to thousands of people over the last forty years of Christian ministry, I've found that one thing is consistent: everyone has faced crisis and disappointment. Listening to people and trading places with them (in our minds) will produce empathy. This is similar to showing compassion. Jesus was moved with compassion before He performed miracles. Compassion compelled Him to reach out to the unreached and unloved. An account in Matthew 9:36–38 summarizes this attitude:

When he saw the crowds, he had compassion for them, because they were harassed and helpless, like sheep without a shepherd. Then he said to his disciples, "The harvest is plentiful, but the laborers are few; therefore pray earnestly to the Lord of the harvest to send out laborers into his harvest."

Jesus called the harassed and helpless people he saw a "harvest." This means that He saw beyond their pain and present crisis and viewed them as reconciled and transformed. This is what the gospel can do in someone's life or in a difficult circumstance. Jesus can still perform miracles today. You are a laborer Jesus is sending out into this harvest!

PAY THE PRICE

After living a perfect life, Jesus Christ announced to His followers that He must suffer and die. He also told them He would be raised from the dead. This was incomprehensible to them. They tried to dissuade Him from thinking this way. How could the greatest man who ever lived suffer such a fate? Some religions believe that Jesus did not die on a Roman cross. They refuse to accept the notion that a prophet of God could be allowed to suffer. Yet Christ was not a prophet. He was God in the flesh.

He came to pay the penalty for the sins of the world. If a law has no penalty for breaking it, it ceases to be a law and becomes a suggestion. God's moral laws have been broken by everyone. God became a man in Christ and suffered in our place.

SEEK

The final principle is a call to go and put all you have learned into practice. Seeking is a big part of being a Christian.

Ask and it will be given to you; seek, and you will find.
(MATTHEW 7:7)

If you truly seek common ground, you will find it.

Whoever diligently seeks good seeks favor, but
evil comes to him who searches for it.
(PROVERBS 11:27)

Jesus announced His mission in a
straightforward statement,

For the Son of Man came to seek and to save the lost.
(LUKE 19:10)

Seeking and saving the lost requires seeking common ground. You must be willing to look for ways to connect with people, seeking to understand their challenges and beliefs. You will need to expend energy and effort to do so. If you lost something important, you would search for it diligently. The greater the value to you, the more urgency will accompany your searching.

SUMMARY

Every believer desiring to share the gospel as well as demonstrate the love of Christ to others must be a common-ground seeker. Finding common ground isn't compromising your beliefs in the name of peace. It is seeking to bring peaceful dialogue where people who don't agree can respectfully share their views. If both parties are really seeking truth, then you as a believer have the opportunity to make the case for Christ.

The STEPS to finding common ground will help guide you and those you influence to open their eyes and expand their horizons to see the multitude of ways where common-ground connections can be made. You will *see* the common ground that exists all around you by intentionally looking for it. *Trading places* helps you alter your viewpoint and develop *empathy*. If you're willing to *pay the price* and partner with others with the same concern for building bridges for the sake of the kingdom, then you can intentionally *seek* not just to find common ground but to utilize it as a launching pad to have a greater impact on the world around you.

1. What is the gospel? Write out the definition given in this chapter.

_____

_____

_____

_____

_____

_____

_____

_____

_____

_____

2. How do we know the gospel is true?

_____

"And if Christ has not been raised, your faith is futile and you are still in your sins."
(1 CORINTHIANS 15:17)

3. The apostle Paul said he became "all things to all people." What goal did he have in mind with this outlook toward others?

_____

"To the weak I became weak, that I might win the weak. I have become all things to all people, that by all means I might save some."

(1 Corinthians 9:22)

4. Christ is now at the right hand of the Father and serves as High Priest on our behalf. How does He respond to our weaknesses (Hebrews 4:15)?

_____

"For we do not have a high priest who is unable to sympathize with our weaknesses, but one who in every respect has been tempted as we are, yet without sin."

(Hebrews 4:15)

5. When two or three are gathered together in Christ's name and on behalf of His mission and message, what does He promise?

_____

"For where two or three are gathered in my name, there am I among them."

(Matthew 18:20)

6. List the STEPS for finding common ground.

_____

_____

_____

_____

_____

7. What are we called to be?

_____

"Therefore be imitators of God, as beloved children."
(Ephesians 5:1

ADDITIONAL LIGHT

"Show hospitality to one another
without grumbling."
(1 PETER 4:9)

"Repentance for the forgiveness of sins
will be preached in his name to all nations,
beginning at Jerusalem."
(LUKE 24:47, NIV)

REFLECTIONS

1. Why is the gospel the ultimate human rights issue?

2. How can you utilize the STEPS to common ground to expand your evangelistic horizon?

3. Who do you know who would be a good partner to work with for a common-ground initiative?

4. Discuss (in a small group setting) areas where common ground can be found.

NOTES

NOTES

NOTES

Dr. Ming Wang, Harvard and MIT (MD, magna cum laude); PhD (laser physics), is a world-renowned eye surgeon, philanthropist, and co-founder of the Tennessee Immigrant and Minority Business Group. He grew up during China's Cultural Revolution during which millions of youth were deported to remote areas to face a life sentence of poverty and hard labor. In 1982, he made his way to the U.S. with only $50, a Chinese-English dictionary, but with a big American dream in his heart. Dr. Wang has published 10 textbooks and over 100 articles, including one in the world-renowned journal "Nature", holds several U.S. patents, including the world's first amniotic membrane contact lens. He received numerous awards including the Honor Award from the American Academy of Ophthalmology, the Lifetime Achievement Award from the Association of Chinese American Physicians, the Kiwanis Nashvillian of the Year Award, NPR's Philanthropist of the Year Award, and an honorary doctorate degree from Trevecca Nazarene University. Dr. Wang founded the Wang Foundation for Sight Restoration which to date has helped patients from over 40 states in the U.S. and from over 55 countries, with all sight restoration surgeries performed free-of-charge. Dr. Wang's autobiography "From Darkness to Sight" has inspired the film "Sight."

Dr. Rice Broocks is a bestselling author of several books including the book "God's Not Dead" that has been translated into 14 languages. He has spoken at universities in over 40 nations. He is the co-founder of Every Nation Churches and Ministries, that operates in 80 nations currently. His doctoral degree is from Fuller Theological Seminary in Pasadena, CA in the field of missiology which focuses on the intersection of the Christian faith and the wide variety of global cultures and beliefs. Dr. Broocks works closely with a team of scientists, philosophers, and historians, that facilitate interdisciplinary dialogue between faith and science.